FAMOUS LIVES

Biographies of famous people to support
the National Curriculum.

Thomas Edison

by Karen Wallace
Illustrations by Peter Kent

W
FRANKLIN WATTS
LONDON•SYDNEY

First published in 1997
by Franklin Watts
This edition 2002

Franklin Watts
96 Leonard Street
London EC2A 4XD

Franklin Watts Australia
56 O'Riordan Street
Alexandria, Sydney
NSW 2015

ISBN 0 7496 4339 0 (pbk)

A CIP catalogue record for this book is
available from the British Library

Dewey Decimal Classification
Number: 608.7

Series Editor: Sarah Ridley
Designer: Kirstie Billingham
Consultant: Dr Anne Millard

Printed in Great Britain

Thomas Edison

Thomas Edison was born in the
United States of America in
1847. He was the last of seven
children. Three died when they
were little.

When he was young he had a bad ear infection which left him slightly deaf. His teachers at school did not understand and thought he was stupid. After a very short time he stopped going to school.

I'll teach you your lessons son. I know you're not stupid.

Thanks, Mother.

Thomas had a lively mind. At home, he tried many strange experiments. He rubbed two cats together to see if their fur would make sparks. One day his mother found him sitting on some goose eggs!

When he was twelve, Thomas worked on the railway selling snacks to passengers. He even printed his own newspaper called *The Weekly Herald*.

WESTERN UNION

BIG BREAK FOR SIXTEEN

YEAR OLD HERO STOP SKY'S

THE LIMIT NOW STOP

One day the station master's
little boy ran onto the tracks.
Thomas grabbed him and saved
his life. As a reward, the station
master taught Thomas how to
use a telegraph machine.

9

Thomas soon started work as a first-class telegraph operator but he wanted to make a machine that would send telegraph messages back and forth at the same time.

It was a brilliant idea but his boss wasn't interested. So Thomas left to become a full-time inventor.

11

When he was twenty-two,
Thomas came up with his first
proper invention. It was called
a stock ticker. It printed out
an endless paper strip of

Stock Market information so people could keep up to date with changes in prices.

He later improved this machine and sold it to a rich business man for $40,000 – a huge sum in those days. With that money, Thomas set up his own company to make his inventions.

Thomas worked long hours and expected his men to do the same. He wasn't interested in making money for its own sake. He was a practical man who loved to solve problems. He said his deafness actually helped him.

16

On Christmas Day in 1871,
Thomas married Mary Stilwell
who was one of his workers. The
story goes that he rushed back to
his workshop only an hour after
his wedding and didn't go home
again until well after midnight.

Mary went on to have three children but their father did not spend much time with them.

Even though Thomas was a sharp bargainer, he was very bad at handling the money he made from his inventions. Dishonest business men cheated him and greedy lawyers took him to court.

Eventually he gave up trying to manufacture his machines and went back to what he knew best.

INVENTING MACHINES!

In 1876 Alexander Bell
invented the telephone but it
had serious problems.

Even if you shouted, the person at the other end could hardly hear because of all the crackle.

A big company called Western Union asked Thomas to solve the problem. It was a difficult job for Thomas because of his deafness but that made him determined to come up with a solution.

In 1878, he invented a transmitter made out of carbon. It was the size of a button and fitted into the telephone. Now a voice could be heard loud and clear. Thomas had invented the first microphone! However, there was one problem.

It was an impossible situation. Western Union decided to sell the rights to Thomas's transmitter to Alexander Bell's company. They made three and a half million dollars.

Thomas made a quarter of a million dollars. He immediately used the money to pay for work on his next invention – an early record player.

The phonograph made Thomas world famous. He showed it to the President of the United States and to great inventors in London.

He even set up a company to make them. But times were hard and the sound wasn't good.

People lost interest in the phonograph so Thomas turned his attention to something else.

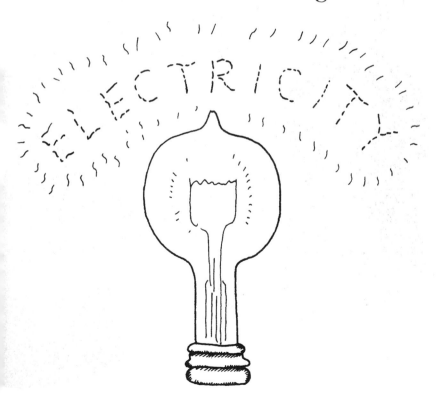

At that time, streets and houses had gas lamps. A few lighthouses used electric light but it was too bright for everyday use.

Thomas wanted to invent a system that would provide electricity to millions of homes and offices.

But there was one huge problem. Thomas needed to invent a long-lasting, low-powered light bulb. He needed to find a substance that would glow when it was heated by electricity. This glow is called *incandescence*. It is what makes all light bulbs bright.

Hastily Thomas made an announcement.

His announcement was reported all over the world. There was only one problem. He hadn't invented the right kind of light bulb. It melted after ten minutes!

Nevertheless, the big companies backed him. After a year of research during which he nearly blinded himself, Thomas came up with the answer.

It's amazing! You just press a button!

But still people believed that
electricity would never take over
from gas. So Thomas moved to
New York, rented a fancy big house
and soon had it blazing with light.

Not only that! He planned to supply a whole area of the city with its own electricity.

And he did!

In 1884, Thomas' first wife died and a year later he married again.

Two years later, Alexander Bell invented a machine called a graphophone which recorded voices onto a wax-coated cylinder.

Thomas looked again at his phonograph. He devised a solid wax cylinder with a floating needle. Within a year he was recording music and making records.

A few years later he had
another brilliant idea. He
invented the first movie camera.
It was called a kinetoscope.

At that time in the 1890s, the first cars began to appear. Thomas thought they could run on electricity and developed a long-lasting storage battery. The battery was used in submarines and ships but not in cars.

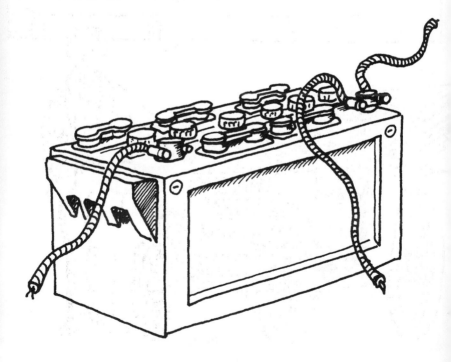

A man who used to work for
Thomas had a better idea.

My name is Henry Ford and this
here is a petrol engine.

Thomas was almost eighty when he retired from his huge business empire. Even though he was very strong, he could not recover from the diabetes and kidney disease that he developed shortly afterwards. He died four years later.

THOMAS
ALVA
EDISON
1847-1931

Further Facts

Big mistakes

Not everything Edison invented was a good idea. He had gigantic failures as well as gigantic successes.
He lost a huge amount of money trying to make a machine that would crush and separate iron ore.

War work

During the First World War, he advised the US government on military machines and invented several devices to fight submarines.

He set up a factory to provide chemicals for his inventions and made more money.

Whose invention is it?

When Thomas invented something he immediately patented it. A patent is a legal document to protect an inventor's idea from being stolen by someone else. By the end of his life, Edison had 389 patents for electric light and power, 195 for the phonograph, 150 for the telegraph, 141 for batteries and 34 for the telephone.

Important dates in Thomas Edison's lifetime

1847   Thomas Edison born in Ohio, USA.

1863   Gets first job as a telegraphist.

1869   Invents stock ticker.

1871   Sets up first factory.

1875   Cheated by business men.

1876   Moves and sets up second factory.

1877   Invents telephone transmitter and phonograph.

1879   Invents electric bulb.

1882   Lights up New York, USA.

1889   Invents kinetoscope and makes the first moving pictures.

1909   Perfects the storage battery.

1914-18 Works for government during First World War.

1922   Nominated *Greatest Living American*.

1931   Dies, aged eighty-four.